About this book

People around the world have been baking and eating bread for thousands of years. The scent of newly baked bread is one of the most recognizable—and inviting—of all cooking smells.

You can bake your own bread, or choose from a wide variety of breads to buy in stores. Whichever you do, one of the easiest and most interesting ways to eat bread is in the form of a sandwich. It may be the club sandwich of the United States, the open-faced sandwich of Scandinavia, or the long, crusty loaf of France.

Cold sandwiches are perfect for picnics, and hot sandwiches are good for lunches, but remember that you can make sandwiches in unusual shapes and with surprising tastes to eat any time.

Choose the sandwich in this book that you want to make, and remember that by changing the kind of bread or the type of filling suggested in the recipe, you can create your own original sandwiches.

First published in the United States of America 1982 by Philomel Books, a division of The Putnam Publishing Group, 200 Madison Avenue, New York, N.Y., 10016. First published in Great Britain 1982 by Methuen Children's Books, Ltd., in association with Walker Books, Ltd., London. Printed in Italy. Cover illustration by Angus Gray-Burbridge

Library of Congress Cataloging in Publication Data
John, Sue.
    The breadbasket cookbook.
    Summary: A guide to baking or buying bread and using it to make a variety of sandwiches for picnics, lunches, and snacks.
    1. Bread—Juvenile literature. [1. Bread.
2. Sandwiches. 3. Cookery] I. Butterworth, Pat, ill.
II. Raymond, Charles, ill. III. Title.
TX769.J58 1982   641.8′4   81-15744
ISBN 0-399-20862-3   AACR2

Contents

The Breadbasket Cookbook

by Sue John
Illustrated by Pat Butterworth
and Charles Raymond

Philomel Books

measuring cup

flour sifter

How to use this book

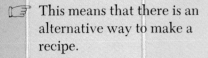 This means that there is an alternative way to make a recipe.

Before you start:
- Wear an apron so that your clothes won't get splashed or stained.
- Read a recipe from start to finish to be sure you have everything you need before you begin.
- Wash your hands before handling food.
- Put all the necessary ingredients on your work surface. If you will be using butter or margarine, be sure that it is soft for spreading.
- Assemble all the cooking equipment you need so that you don't have to stop in the middle of a recipe to find something.
- Use a kitchen timer, if you have one, to ensure proper cooking times.

While you cook:
- Always use pot holders or oven mitts when handling hot pots or pans.
- Pick up a knife by its handle, not by its blade.
- Keep your work surface as neat as possible, so that you can see what you are doing.

- If anything spills on the floor, mop it up immediately to avoid accidents.

After you finish:
- Put away any unused ingredients.
- Wash, dry and put away all your equipment.
- Clean your work surface.

Preparing salad foods:
- Wash salad ingredients and fruits with skins before you use them. The important point to remember is never to soak food. Shake off any excess water immediately.
- The easiest way to wash fruits and vegetables is to put them in a colander and run cold water over them.
- Other vegetables, such as celery or carrots, might need to be scrubbed with a small brush under cold, running water.
- To clean lettuce, wash each leaf separately with cold water. Put the leaves into a colander as you wash them. Shake off any excess water.

Helpful hints:
- When slicing bread for sandwiches, cut thin slices so that you can eat the sandwiches easily. Don't cut off crusts—they help to keep the bread fresh.
- When making sandwiches, spread butter or margarine on the bread to prevent the fillings from soaking into it and making it soggy. Use a table knife to spread it, and be generous.
- When you make sandwiches with different fillings at the same time, use a clean knife or spoon to spread each different filling.
- When you have made sandwiches, use a bread knife to cut them in half.
- When cutting herbs, use a pair of scissors instead of a knife.
- When using the broiler, turn it to its maximum heat and wait until it is hot before putting food in to broil. Watch constantly to be sure food doesn't burn.

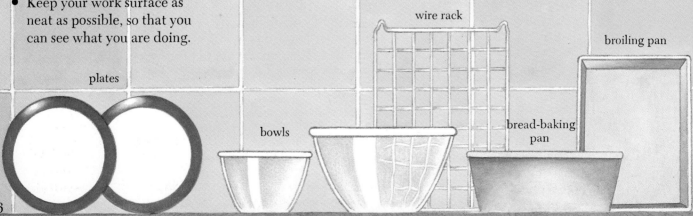
plates

wire rack

bowls

broiling pan

bread-baking pan

colander   pastry cutters   saucepan   grater

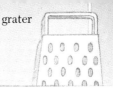

How to measure

The system of measurement used in the United States is different from the metric system most countries use. In the U.S. the liquid measure of one cup is used to measure both liquid and dry ingredients. The metric system measures dry ingredients by weight (grams and kilograms) and liquids by milliliters and liters. Grams are abbreviated g and liters are abbreviated l.

Liquid measure

U.S.	Metric
1 oz. (ounce)	about 30 milliliters
½ cup	about 120 milliliters
1 cup (½ pint)	about ¼ liter
1 quart	about 1 liter

Dry measure

U.S.	Metric
1 oz. (ounce)	about 28 grams
1 pound	about 450 grams

Dry ingredients can be measured in tablespoons, too. One heaping tablespoon of flour amounts to 25 grams of flour.

How to use the stove

Be careful whenever you use the stove. Always use pot holders or oven mitts when handling hot pots and pans. Be sure to turn oven and stove dials to "off" when you have finished cooking.

Each recipe will tell you the correct temperature at which to set your oven. Be sure to preheat the oven to the temperature called for in the recipe before putting food in to bake. Allow 15 or 20 minutes for the oven to preheat. Fahrenheit is abbreviated F.

Equipment

This is a list of all the cooking equipment you will need for the recipes in this book. Always ask an adult or older friend for help if you aren't sure how to use something.

A few explanations:

Bread board: always use this when slicing or cutting bread.

Bread knife: used to slice bread and cut sandwiches.

Cheese slicer: used to cut thin slices of cheese from a chunk of cheese.

Chopping board: always use this when cutting, chopping or slicing ingredients.

Garlic press: used to crush garlic cloves.

Grater: used to break food into small pieces. Watch your knuckles when you use a grater!

Pastry brush: used in this book to spread olive oil and to brush the tops of bread rolls.

aluminum foil
bread-baking pans
bread board
broiling pan
can opener
cheese slicer
chopping board
colander
cookie sheets (two)
dishcloth
dish towels
drinking straws
flour sifter
forks
frying pan (small)
garlic press
glasses
grater
knives:
    bread
    large, sharp
    small, sharp
    table

measuring cups
measuring spoons
mixing bowls:
    large
    small
oven mitts
paper towels
pastry brush
pastry cutters
plastic bags and
    containers
plates (different sizes)
pot holders
saucepan (small)
scissors
spatula
spoons:
    table
    tea
    wooden
toaster
vegetable brush
wire rack

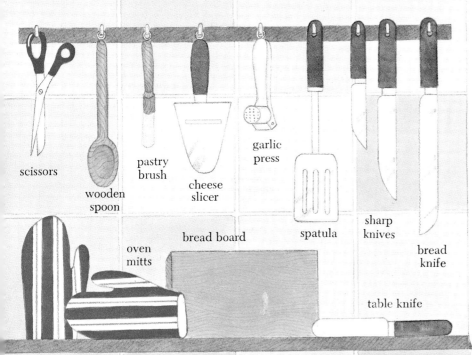

scissors

wooden spoon

pastry brush

cheese slicer

garlic press

spatula

sharp knives

bread knife

oven mitts

bread board

table knife

Breads to bake or buy

Breads to buy

You can bake your own bread (see pp. 10-13) or buy it in a store. Bread comes in all shapes and sizes, colors and flavors. One reason for this is that different countries around the world bake their breads using flour made from local crops, such as wheat, rye, corn, buckwheat, barley and millet. No two flours look or taste exactly alike, and neither do the breads baked from them. Shop around in your local stores to see the wide range of breads available. Bread is good for you—it contains vitamins and minerals that your body needs. It is a staple food around the world, even though the bread baked in some countries may look quite different from the bread you are used to seeing and eating!

Packaged, sliced bread is good for toasting, frying and making sandwiches. White, light rye, whole wheat and other crusty loaves can be used for sandwiches, and are delicious eaten just with

butter. Dark rye, pumpernickel and brown breads are particularly good for "open-faced" sandwiches (see pp. 24-25).

And a sandwich that is delicious as well as nutritious can also be made with pita or Arab bread which is sold in many large supermarkets and food specialty stores.

Some breads, such as the long, thin, crusty loaves and rolls, should be eaten on the day you buy them. You can keep other loaves fresh for two days if you put them in a breadbox, or wrap them in a plastic bag and put them in the refrigerator. Bread that you buy wrapped can be kept for three days in a breadbox or refrigerator or can be frozen for later use.

Experiment with various breads when you make sandwiches. The fillings will taste different with different kinds of breads.

Bread to bake

Bread is exciting to bake—it is fun to knead, wonderful to smell, magical to watch and delicious to eat! Before you begin, read the baking hints on page 12.

Ingredients

450 g all-purpose flour
2 level teaspoons salt
25 g soft butter or margarine
15 g fresh yeast
1 level teaspoon sugar
300 ml warm water
small piece of butter

1. Sift the flour and salt into a large mixing bowl.

2. Using a small, sharp knife, cut the butter into small pieces. Drop them into the bowl. With your fingers rub the flour and butter together until the butter disappears.

6. Sprinkle some flour over your work surface. Dip your hands into the flour and lift the dough from the bowl onto the floured surface.

7. Knead the dough for five minutes by pushing the heels of your hands into the dough and away from your body.

8. Fold the dough back over toward you and push again. Turn the dough as you knead so that every part is pushed and pulled. If necessary, add a little more flour to the work surface.

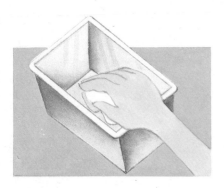

12. Holding a small piece of butter in a piece of paper towel, rub it all around the inside of a bread-baking pan.

13. Lift the dough into the baking pan, pushing gently with your fingertips until all the dough fits inside. Then preheat the oven to 425°F.

14. Leave the baking pan in a warm place for about 25 minutes, until the dough has risen to the top of the pan.

3. Put the yeast and sugar into a small mixing bowl. Using a teaspoon, stir them until the yeast turns runny. Slowly add the warm water and use the teaspoon to stir it in.

4. Using a wooden spoon, press a hole in the middle of the flour and butter mixture. Pour the runny yeast mixture into this hole, and stir well.

5. Stir the dough around until everything is well mixed. The sides of the bowl should be almost clean. If the dough seems too soft and sticky, add a little flour. If it's dry, add more water.

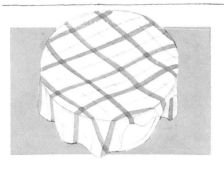

9. Sprinkle flour into a large, clean mixing bowl. Lift the dough into the bowl. Run a clean dish towel under hot water, wring it out and drape it over the bowl.

10. Leave the bowl in a warm place (a warm kitchen cupboard or near a radiator) until the dough has risen to twice its original size. This will take about 1½ -2 hours.

11. Repeat steps 6-8.

15. Put the pan into the middle of the hot oven and bake for 35-40 minutes until the loaf is golden brown.

16. Using oven mitts, carefully remove the pan from the oven and put it onto a wooden surface. Let it sit for 10 minutes.

17. Put a wire rack on top of the pan. Turn them both upside down. Lift off the pan and turn the loaf right side up to cool.

Bread braids

1. You can shape the basic bread dough into braided rolls—these are especially good for picnics. At step 11 (see p. 11), after repeating steps 6-8, cut the dough into 12 equal pieces.

2. Cut one of these pieces into three equal pieces. Roll each into a strip about 10 cm long. Put the three strips alongside each other and pinch the tops together.

3. Weave the strips together to form a braid. Pinch the bottom ends together. Repeat steps 2-3 on this page with the other 11 pieces of dough.

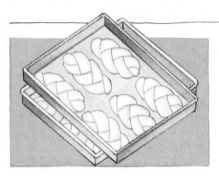

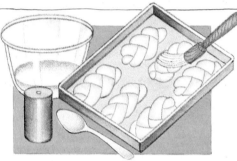

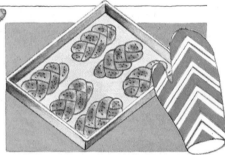

4. Grease two cookie sheets (see step 12, p. 10). Put the rolls, slightly apart, onto the cookie sheets. Leave them in a warm place for 20 minutes, so that the dough can rise.

5. If you want crusty rolls, mix two level teaspoons of salt with two tablespoons of hot water in a bowl. Using a pastry brush, paint the mixture lightly over the rolls.

6. You can sprinkle poppy or sesame seeds, cracked wheat or crushed cornflakes over the rolls. Bake in an oven heated to 425° F. for 20 minutes, remove the cookie sheets and let the rolls cool.

Baking hints

- Rest the mixing bowl on a damp cloth to keep it from slipping.
- Fresh yeast is easier to use, but you can also use dried yeast. Follow directions on the packet.
- Yeast needs certain conditions to grow. A warm bowl, wooden working surface, wooden spoon and warm hands all help create the correct conditions.

- The water must not be too hot, or it will kill the live organisms in the yeast before it starts to grow.
- The more thoroughly you knead the dough, the lighter your baked bread will be.
- The hot, wet cloth that you put over the bowl while the dough is rising helps speed up the rising process.

- To be sure that your bread is thoroughly baked, turn the loaf upside down on the palm of one hand (wear an oven mitt!) and tap it with the knuckles of your other hand. It should sound hollow.
- For a light brown, rough-textured loaf, use a mixture of 225 g whole-wheat flour and 225 g white flour in the basic recipe on pp. 10-11.

Garlic bread

Served warm, garlic bread is especially delicious with a salad or other cold foods. The flavor of garlic is strong, so don't use more garlic cloves than the recipe calls for. A loaf of French or Italian bread this size will feed 4 to 6 people. Preheat oven to 375°F.

Ingredients

1 long, crusty, white loaf
    about 50 cm long
100 g softened butter
3 garlic cloves
salt and pepper

1. Holding the loaf on its side, use a bread knife to make diagonal cuts about 2 cm apart along the whole loaf. The cuts should slice almost through to the other side.

2. Put the butter onto a plate. Use the flat side of a table knife to soften the butter.

3. Peel off the garlic skins. Using a garlic press, crush the cloves into a bowl. Or, using the flat blade of a table knife, squash the cloves on a plate and use the juice.

4. Add the crushed cloves of garlic or the juice to the butter. Season with a little salt and pepper. Use the knife to blend everything together.

5. Holding the slices of bread apart with one hand, carefully use the knife to spread equal amounts of the garlic butter onto one side of each slice.

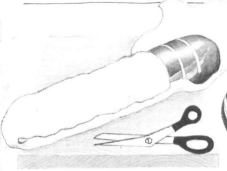

6. Using scissors, cut out a piece of aluminum foil about 50 cm x 30 cm. Put the loaf onto the foil so that it is resting on its uncut side. Wrap the foil around the loaf.

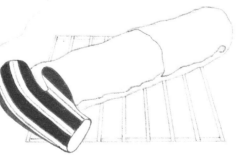

7. Using oven mitts, put the wrapped loaf into the center of the oven and bake for 20 minutes.

8. Carefully put the wrapped loaf onto a large plate or bread board. Taking care not to burn yourself, open the foil and serve at once.

Picnic sandwiches

Sandwiches and picnics are made for each other! It is easy to pack a picnic of sandwiches and set off to the park, country or seaside. Sandwiches are so quick to make that you can prepare a picnic at very short notice. Fresh air makes you hungry, so take along plenty to eat.

You can make picnic sandwiches using your favorite bread or rolls. The choice of fillings is endless—you can make a sandwich out of almost any food you enjoy. Sandwiches can be made in advance—even the night before the picnic, as long as you wrap them properly to keep them fresh. You can use foil, self-sticking plastic wrap or plastic bags. Wrap them tightly and neatly so that the fillings cannot fall out. It's best to do this as soon as you make them, to keep the bread from hardening and curling up at the edges. Wrap sandwiches that have different fillings separately, to keep the flavors separate. Keep wrapped sandwiches in the refrigerator until it is time to pack your picnic basket.

On a picnic it is important to take just what you need. If you are going for a walk or a bicycle ride, you will want to carry as little as possible. Two neatly wrapped sandwiches, a celery stick and a crisp apple should be enough to keep you going.

However, if you are going to be out for a whole day, it's a good idea to make a list of everything you want to take. Here is a sample list.

- sandwiches; two different types, and at least one sandwich for each person, neatly wrapped and sealed in plastic bags
- washed carrot sticks, celery and tomatoes in plastic bags
- popcorn or potato chips in plastic bags
- cake or cookies in firm plastic containers
- fruit in a firm plastic container
- drinks in plastic bottles or a thermos
- paper cups and plates, plastic spoons and a knife
- napkins or paper towels
- damp cloth for sticky fingers, in a plastic bag
- a blanket
- antiseptic cream and adhesive bandages
- large plastic bag for garbage

When packing a large picnic, put everything on the kitchen table first. If you don't have a picnic hamper, choose a basket that isn't too deep—a sturdy wicker one is ideal. Put the food that is in firm plastic containers at the bottom of the basket. Keep all drinks upright. Wrap the spoons and knife in a dish towel or put them in a bag. Put the lightweight foods on top so they won't get squashed.

To secure the food in an open basket, gently cover the top with a clean dish towel and tuck the edges inside the basket. Check your list to be sure that you have everything—double-check the refrigerator to be sure that you have not forgotten the sandwiches!

Fisherman's snack

These sandwiches will satisfy the hungriest group of friends on a day's outing. Hard-boiled eggs go well with many other ingredients besides tuna, so you might want to try some variations of your own. This recipe makes 4 sandwiches.

Ingredients

8 slices buttered bread
2 eggs
1 small can tuna fish
2-3 tablespoons mayonnaise
salt and pepper

1. Fill a small saucepan halfway with cold water. Using a tablespoon, carefully put in the eggs. Bring the water to a gentle boil and cook eggs for seven minutes. Turn off the heat.

2. Use the spoon to lift out the eggs and put them in a bowl of cold water for fifteen minutes.

3. Remove the eggs one at a time and tap the shells gently on the rim of the bowl. Peel off and discard the shells and outer skins.

4. Using a small, sharp knife, slice the eggs. Arrange the egg slices on four slices of bread.

5. Open the can of tuna and drain off the oil. Empty the tuna into a small, clean bowl. Add the mayonnaise, salt and pepper. Use a fork to mash everything together.

☞ You can use natural yogurt instead of mayonnaise. Add lettuce leaves or cucumber slices, too, if you like.

6. Spread the tuna mixture on top of the egg slices.

7. Cover the ingredients with the four remaining slices of bread.

Cool, crisp cheese

Soft cream cheese and crunchy celery are a delicious combination, particularly in a sandwich made with a rough-textured brown bread such as whole-wheat. This recipe feeds 4 people, and tastes just as good as it looks.

Ingredients

100 g cream cheese
2-3 celery sticks
salt and pepper
8 slices buttered brown bread
watercress

1. Using a tablespoon, put the cream cheese into a small bowl.

2. With a small, sharp knife, chop up the celery into small pieces. Throw out any "stringy" pieces.

3. Put the celery into the bowl. Using a fork, mix everything together. Season with a little salt and pepper.

4. Using a table knife, spread the mixture onto four slices of the bread.

5. Put a few sprigs of watercress on top of each.

6. Cover the ingredients with the four remaining slices of bread.

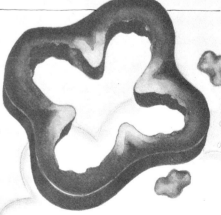

☞ Try chopped walnuts instead of celery, or thin slices of pepper rings instead of watercress.

Picnic loaf

This sandwich uses one whole loaf of French or Italian bread, which should be about 50 cm long to feed 4 to 6 people. When you are ready to eat, cut it into individual portions and serve.

Ingredients

1 long, crusty, white loaf about
    50 cm long
olive oil
1 small, green pepper
2 firm tomatoes
8 thin salami slices
chunk of cheddar cheese, about
    150 g
salt and pepper

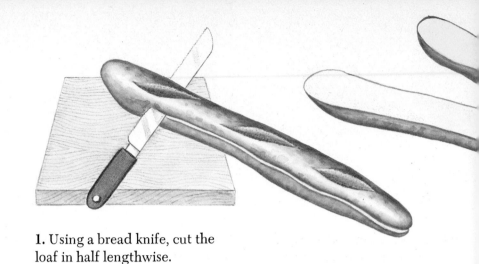

1. Using a bread knife, cut the loaf in half lengthwise.

5. Put a layer of salami slices on the bottom half of the loaf.

6. Put a layer of pepper rings on top of the salami slices.

7. Put a layer of cheese slices on top of the pepper rings.

Country crunch

Use a rough-textured brown bread when you make this sandwich, for a nut-like taste. This recipe feeds 4 people.

Ingredients

100 g cottage cheese
small bunch chives
salt and pepper
8 slices buttered brown bread
1 large, firm tomato
½ cucumber

1. Put the cottage cheese into a small bowl. Using scissors, finely snip the chives into the bowl. Season with a little salt and pepper.

2. Using a fork, mix together the cheese and chives. Use a table knife to spread the mixture onto four slices of the bread.

2. Pour a little olive oil into a cup. Dip a pastry brush into it and spread a little oil onto the insides of both halves of the open loaf.

3. Using a small, sharp knife, cut the pepper into thin rings. Cut out the inside seeds and throw them out. Cut the tomatoes into thin slices.

4. Remove the skins from the salami slices and throw them out. Remove the rind from the cheese and use a cheese slicer to cut off eight thin slices.

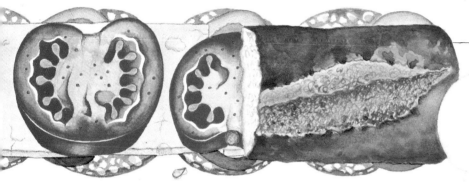

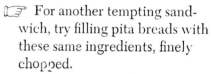

8. Put a layer of tomato slices on top of the cheese slices. Season with salt and pepper.

9. Cover the ingredients with the top half of the loaf.

☞ For another tempting sandwich, try filling pita breads with these same ingredients, finely chopped.

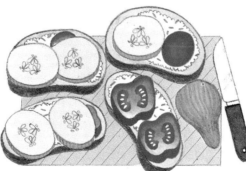

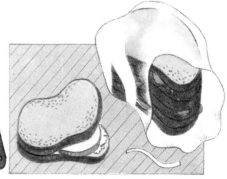

3. Using a small, sharp knife, cut the tomato into thin slices. Put the slices on top of the mixture of cheese and chives.

4. Using a small, sharp knife, cut the cucumber half into thin slices. Arrange them on top of the tomato slices.

5. Cover the ingredients with the four remaining slices of bread.

Lunchtime sandwiches

Sandwiches taste even more delicious when they are attractively served. If you are having guests, make the table look inviting so that you will enjoy sitting, eating and talking there. Set the table with plates for the sandwiches and for a dessert of fresh fruit. Don't forget forks, knives and spoons, glasses, and a jug filled with an iced drink. You can float ice cubes and perhaps a slice of lemon in the drink just before serving it.

Be sure to put salt and pepper shakers on the table, as well as small bowls of ketchup, pickles, mustard or relish.

Serve interesting salads of your favorite ingredients. Use lettuce as a base, and add cucumber chunks, pepper-slices, a pile of grated carrots, a few raisins, with chopped parsley or mint sprinkled over everything. Serve with mayonnaise or your favorite salad dressing.

Try cutting radish or tomato roses—they look pretty and taste good.

Use a small, sharp knife to cut off the stalks and "tails" of the radishes. Holding a radish in one hand, make cuts all around the middle of the radish. The bottom of each cut must touch the one next to it and should slant in the opposite direction to it. Make the cuts deep enough so that each radish separates into two roses. Make tomato roses in a similar way.

If you want to decorate your food with lemon twists, use a small, sharp knife to cut a lemon into slices. Make one cut into the center of each slice. Pick up a slice in two hands, so that a thumb and index finger of each hand is holding the rind on either side of the cut. Twist your hands in opposite directions, up and down, to make the lemon twist.

Arrange your dessert of washed fruit in a bowl as your centerpiece. Put firm fruits, such as apples and oranges, at the bottom, and the smaller, softer fruits, such as cherries or apricots, on top.

If you are eating alone, your meal will be more enjoyable if you serve it nicely. You can cover a tray with a small, brightly colored cloth, add a tall glass with a straw for your drink and a plate for your sandwich, as well as a small salad.

Hot sandwiches can change an ordinary lunch into a special one. They are ideal for a weekend or holiday treat because they are best eaten while crisp and warm.

Here is an easy recipe for a hot sandwich. To make melted cheese sandwiches, put two or three slices of processed American cheese on a slice of buttered bread. Use a table knife to spread a little relish or mustard over the cheese. Cover the ingredients with another slice of buttered bread.

Melt about 20 g of butter in a small frying pan, over low heat, until the butter starts to bubble. Using a spatula, carefully put the sandwich into the pan. Fry for one minute. Slide the spatula under the sandwich and turn it over in the pan. Fry on that side for one minute. Both sides should be a light golden brown. If you fry more sandwiches, add more butter to the pan.

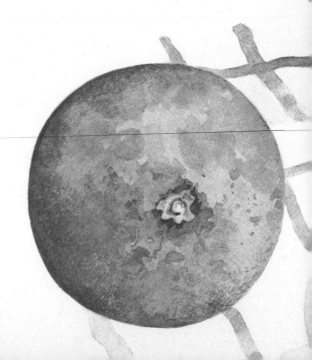

Everyday munchies

If you take your lunch to school, vary the type of bread and the filling from day to day, so that you can look forward to new tastes. Round off your meal with a dessert of fresh fruit. After you have tried this recipe, invent your own everyday sandwiches.

Ingredients
2 slices Colby or cheddar cheese
brown or white buttered roll
peanut butter
handful of raisins

1. Put the slices of cheese onto the bottom half of the roll.

2. Using a table knife, spread peanut butter over the cheese.

3. Sprinkle the raisins over the peanut butter. Cover the ingredients with the top half of the roll.

☞ You don't have to use expensive fillings in your everyday sandwiches. With a little imagination, you can make exciting sandwiches using leftover cold meats and salad ingredients. Try making sandwiches using three different ingredients in each one. Use lettuce, thin slices of pork and sliced tomatoes; or peanut butter, thin slices of chicken and watercress. Ham, cucumber and relish taste good together, and so do lettuce, thin slices of turkey and a pepper ring. You can use mayonnaise or plain yogurt instead of butter. Remember to season well with salt and pepper, and add mustard for an extra-tangy taste.

Super club

This is a filling sandwich to eat, because it is made with three slices of bread. You can use any leftover cold meats in this sandwich.

Ingredients

1 firm tomato
3 slices white bread
butter or margarine
2 lettuce leaves
1 slice cooked ham
1 slice cooked chicken
watercress
1 heaping teaspoon mayonnaise

1. Using a small, sharp knife, cut the tomato into thin slices.

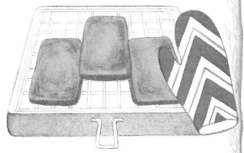

2. Toast the bread in a toaster or, if you like, you can broil it in your broiler. If you use the broiler, watch the toast carefully to be sure it doesn't burn. Toast both sides to a light brown.

3. Put the toast onto a wooden board. Using a table knife, spread butter over one side of each slice.

4. Put the lettuce, ham and tomato slices onto one slice of buttered toast.

5. Cover the ingredients with a second slice of toast, buttered side up.

6. Put the chicken and watercress onto the top slice of toast. Use the teaspoon to add mayonnaise.

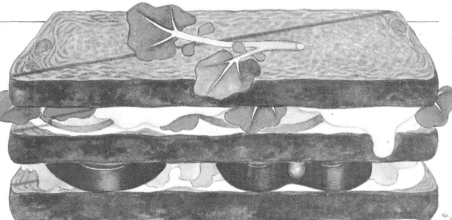

7. Cover all the ingredients with the third slice of toast. Pressing down gently with one hand, carefully use a bread knife to cut the sandwich diagonally in half.

Toasted sardine special

This sandwich is very quick to make. Toasting any sandwich changes the texture of the filling so that ordinary sandwiches taste and look quite special. This recipe makes one sandwich.

Ingredients

1 can skinless and boneless
   sardines
2 slices buttered brown bread
1 tomato
pepper

1. Preheat the broiler. Put 2 of the sardines into a small bowl. Use a fork to mash them. Using a table knife, spread the sardines onto one slice of the bread.

2. Using a small, sharp knife, cut the tomato into thin slices.

Open-faced sandwiches

A tray full of these sandwiches makes a delicious lunch. Use your favorite breads as the bases, and add radish roses or lemon twists (see p. 20).

Ingredients

1 egg
1 slice buttered pumpernickel
   bread
2 thin tomato slices
1 small onion

1. Hard-boil the egg, allow it to cool and remove the shell (see p. 16).

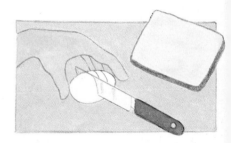

2. Hold the "ends" of the egg between a thumb and middle finger. Using a small, sharp knife, slice the egg downwards. Put the slices onto the bread.

☞ Other tasty combinations for open-faced sandwiches would be: lettuce, sweet corn, black grapes and parsley, or salami and cucumber slices with radishes.

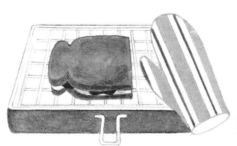

3. Put a layer of tomato slices on top of the sardines. Season with a little pepper.

4. Cover the ingredients with the other slice of bread. Carefully put the sandwich onto the broiler pan. Toast one side a light, golden brown.

5. Use the spatula to turn the sandwich over. Toast that side the same color. Use the spatula to lift the sandwich carefully onto a plate.

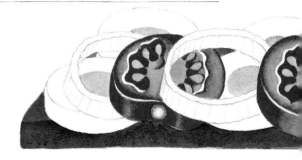

3. Peel off the outer skin of the onion. Using a small, sharp knife, thinly slice the onion. Use your finger to push apart the slices so that they separate into rings.

4. Put a few onion rings on top of the egg slices so that the rings overlap each other.

5. Arrange the tomato slices on top of the onion rings.

☞ You could also try chicken slices, mayonnaise, radishes, mustard and watercress, or slices of smoked fish with green pepper rings and lemon slices.

Surprise sandwiches

Surprise sandwiches are fun to eat any time—on picnics, for lunch, for parties or just when you feel like having a special snack. Treat your friends to some Fresh fruit fancies (see pp. 28-29) or some Butterscotch fingers (see p. 28). Try chocolate sprinkles on fingers of buttered bread—this looks and tastes wonderful! After you try these ideas, look through the refrigerator, food cupboard or fruit bowl to make your own surprises.

Surprise sandwiches must look exciting and taste amazing. Use a sharp knife to cut out simple shapes, such as rectangles or triangles, from your prepared sandwiches. Or use pastry cutters to make your shapes before you prepare the sandwiches. It's best not to use fancy cutters, because the bread won't come out of them easily. Use round cutters to make circular shapes; cut them again for half-moon shapes. If you are giving a party, make the shapes of your sandwiches relate to the theme—round sandwiches can be records, for a disco party, and moons are good for a Halloween party.

Make funny faces on round sandwiches by adding grated carrot for hair, raisins for eyes, small pieces of tomato or radish for noses and mouths. See which ingredients will make faces that look most like your friends or family!

You can make a surprise butter for your sand-

26

wiches, too. The surprise is in the taste. Use flavored butters on open, closed, hot or cold sandwiches.

Certain flavored butters taste better with some ingredients than with others. After you try these, create your own. Whichever flavor you decide to make, use the flat blade of a table knife to blend the ingredients into the soft butter on a small plate.

You can make mint butter by adding two tablespoons of finely snipped mint and a little salt and pepper to 50 g of butter. Use this on a sandwich with hard-boiled eggs, such as Fisherman's snack (see p. 16).

Make chive butter by adding two tablespoons of finely snipped chives and a little salt and pepper to 50 g of butter. Use this with cheese, ham, or on an open-faced sandwich (see p. 24).

You can also make parsley, tarragon or thyme butter in the same way. Parsley butter tastes good with fish. Use tarragon or thyme butter with chicken or turkey.

To make lemon butter, add the finely grated rind of one lemon to 10 g of butter. Use this on a fish sandwich.

Add a little tomato ketchup to 50 g of butter for tomato butter. Use this on cold meat sandwiches.

Don't forget that you can flavor cream cheese in the same way.

Fresh fruit fancies

These sandwiches are so delicious they will probably disappear as quickly as you can make them.

Ingredients
2 slices brown bread spread with cream cheese
fresh strawberries
2 slices buttered white bread covered with chocolate spread
2 slices buttered white bread
fresh raspberries
1 level teaspoon sugar

Strawberry delight
1. Use a small, sharp knife to cut small strawberries in half. Cut large strawberries into slices 1 cm thick.

2. Cover one slice of brown bread spread with cream cheese with the strawberry slices.

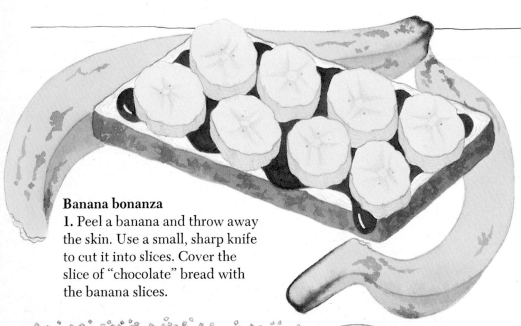

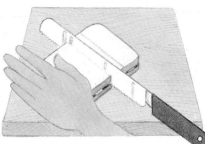

Banana bonanza
1. Peel a banana and throw away the skin. Use a small, sharp knife to cut it into slices. Cover the slice of "chocolate" bread with the banana slices.

2. Cover the ingredients with another slice of "chocolate" bread. Pressing down gently with one hand, use a bread knife to cut the sandwich into finger shapes.

Melting moments

When you put brown sugar or marshmallows under the broiler for a moment, they change as if by magic! Watch them the whole time they cook—the magic happens very quickly. Remember: when using the broiler wear oven mitts to protect your hands!

Ingredients
2 slices buttered bread
1 level tablespoon brown sugar
about 5 marshmallows

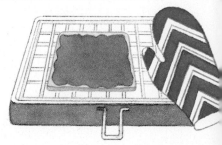

Butterscotch fingers
1. Sprinkle the tablespoon of sugar over one slice of bread.

2. Put the slice of bread on a broiling pan and put the pan under the broiler. Broil until the sugar melts—about one minute.

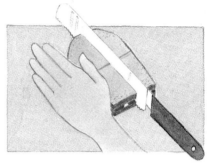

3. Cover the ingredients with the other slice of bread. Pressing down gently with one hand, use a bread knife to cut the sandwich into squares.

Raspberry dream

1. Cover one slice of white bread with raspberries and sprinkle with the sugar.

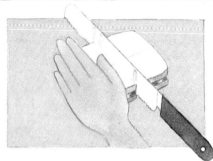

2. Cover the ingredients with the other slice of bread. Pressing down gently with one hand, use a bread knife to cut the sandwich into squares.

3. Use a spatula to lift the bread onto a wooden board. Using a large, sharp knife, cut the bread into finger shapes. Arrange them on a plate.

Marshmallow bubbles

1. Using a small, sharp knife, cut the marshmallows in half and put them onto a slice of bread. Put it on a broiler pan and carefully put the pan under the broiler.

2. Broil for a moment until the marshmallows begin to melt and turn brown on top. Use a spatula to lift up the bread and put it onto a plate.

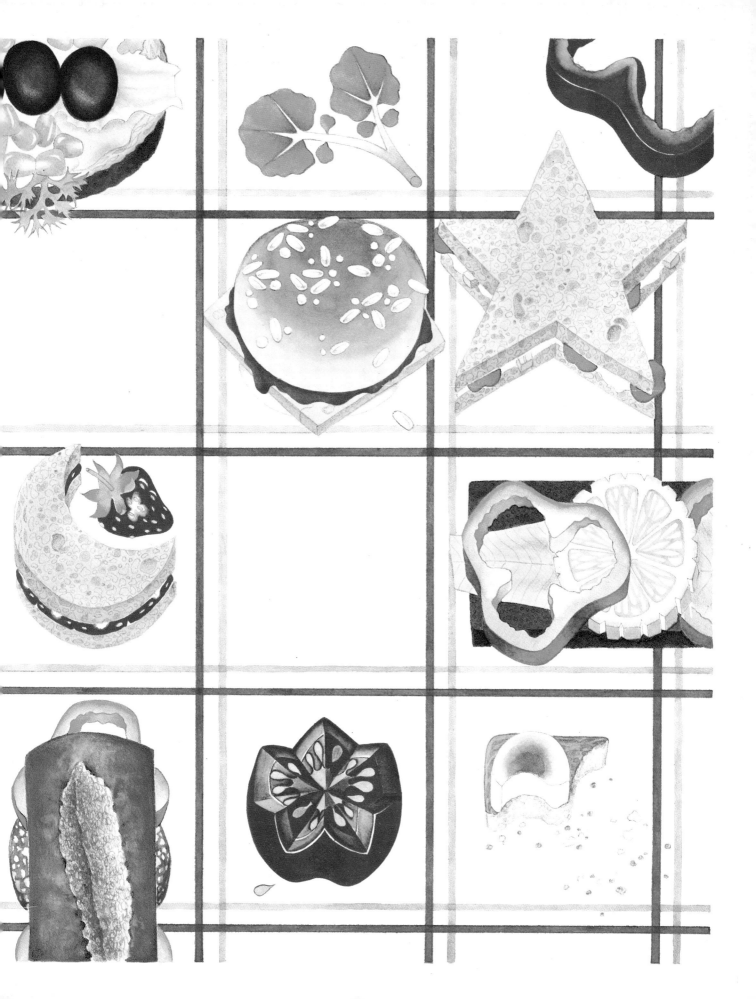